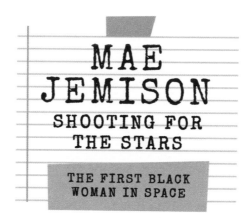

MAE JEMISON

SHOOTING FOR THE STARS

THE FIRST BLACK WOMAN IN SPACE

Published by Bushel & Peck Books, a family-run publishing house in Fresno, California, that believes in uplifting children with the highest standards of art, music, literature, and ideas. Find beautiful books for gifted young minds at www.bushelandpeckbooks.com.

Type set in LTC Kennerley Pro, Special Elite, Nexa Rust Sans, Josefin Sans, and AltaCalifornia.

Bushel & Peck Books is dedicated to fighting illiteracy all over the world. For every book we sell, we donate one to a child in need—book for book. To nominate a school or organization to receive free books, please visit www.bushelandpeckbooks.com.

LCCN: 2023951171

ISBN: 978-1-63819-178-0

First Edition

Printed in China

1 3 5 7 9 10 8 6 4 2

BLACK HISTORY HEROES

MAE JEMISON
SHOOTING FOR THE STARS

THE FIRST BLACK WOMAN IN SPACE

CHRIS SINGLETON WITH RYAN G. VAN CLEAVE

ILLUSTRATED BY ADRIANA PÉREZ PERALES

MILK + COOKIES

Contents

Dedicated to the memory of the victims of the Mother Emanuel Church Tragedy:

REV. SHARONDA COLEMAN-SINGLETON
REV. CLEMENTA PINCKNEY
CYNTHIA GRAHAM HURD
SUSIE JACKSON
ETHEL LANCE
REV. DEPAYNE MIDDLETON-DOCTOR
TYWANZA SANDERS
REV. DANIEL SIMMONS
MYRA THOMPSON
& SURVIVORS

1

Blast Off with Mae Jemison

I like to think of ideas as potential energy. They're really wonderful, but nothing will happen until we risk putting them into action.

—MAE JEMISON

Are you ready for an out-of-this-world adventure? Prepare for liftoff as we rocket through the life of the one and only Mae Jemison, a fearless pioneer who dared to dream big and reach for the stars. Buckle up, because this thrilling journey has the A-OK to launch!

From the start, Mae seemed destined to make history. But her journey wasn't always smooth sailing. Growing up during a time when African Americans and women faced many challenges and discrimination, Mae knew that she would have to work extra hard to achieve her goals.

And guess what? She did just that! Mae's family moved to Chicago when she was young, and it was there that her passion for science truly ignited. In her new home, Mae found inspiration in her surroundings and developed a deep curiosity for the unknown. She would often gaze up at the night sky, wondering what mysteries lay beyond the twinkling stars.

As a young girl, Mae was fascinated by the world around her. She loved to explore, learn new things, and ask questions about everything she encountered. With the support of her family, Mae dove into her studies, devouring books on science, history, and more. She had a particular love for astronomy and the idea of traveling through space.

Mae's incredible journey led her to become a super-smart, multi-talented **trailblazer**. She excelled in school, studying chemical engineering at Stanford University (talk about impressive!) and later earning a medical degree from Cornell University. Thanks to her brains and determination, she had the chance to travel the world, providing healthcare to those in need, and she even served as a Peace Corps medical officer in West Africa.

But Mae's heart belonged to the stars, and she knew that becoming an astronaut was her ultimate goal. In 1987, her dreams finally took flight when she was accepted into the astronaut program run by the National Aeronautics and Space Administration (NASA). After years of intense training, Mae Jemison boarded the Space Shuttle *Endeavour* on September 12, 1992, and made history as

the first Black woman to travel to space! How awesome is that?

During her time at NASA, Mae not only made history, but she also contributed to important space missions and research. She puts her smarts to work on various projects, such as conducting experiments on the effects of weightlessness on the human body and investigating new materials for use in space. Mae's **innovative** work paved the way for future space exploration and helped us understand more about the universe we live in.

Mae's amazing adventure didn't stop there. After her history-making spaceflight, she continued to break barriers and inspire future generations. From founding an international science camp for kids to working on groundbreaking projects that merge science and technology, Mae's legacy continues to soar well beyond the stars.

And what about her life beyond space? Well, Mae Jemison is nothing short of WOW there, too! She's a dancer and a writer, and she even dabbled in acting. With such a wide range of talents, Mae's life is a perfect example of how passion, dedication, and hard work can lead to incredible achievements.

So, get ready to be dazzled by Mae's incredible journey and find out how she traveled to space, defied the odds, and left a lasting impact on the world. This is one cosmic adventure you won't want to miss!

WORDS TO KNOW

trailblazer: A person who makes a new pathway through wild country or is the first to do something exciting or different.

innovative: Introducing new ideas; being creative and original.

THE WORLD AT THE TIME

In 1956:

- Dr. Seuss' *The Cat in the Hat* is published.
- the first episode of *The Price Is Right* airs on television.
- the United States's first attempt to launch a satellite, Vanguard TV3, fails.

WHAT DO YOU THINK?

- What do you think inspired Mae to have such huge dreams despite facing challenges and discrimination?
- Which of Mae's many accomplishments do you think she's most proud of?

2

The Cosmic Kid: An Out-of-this-World Childhood

At camp I remember looking at the stars
. . . and drifting completely away. It was that
sense of drifting away, yet belonging fully to the
universe, that would take me to the library over
and over again to learn more about the stars.

—MAE JEMISON

Let's travel back to the 1960s, when a little girl named Mae Carol Jemison was just beginning her journey to the stars.

She was born on October 17, 1956, in Decatur, Alabama, but here's the hard truth—her family struggled. Her mother, Dorothy, didn't complete college, but she worked hard to care for her family and she occasionally cleaned homes or sewed clothes for money. Her father, Charlie, was a roofer, sweating away on ladders and roofs and handling hot tar and shingles.

A lot of Black families in the South struggled as well at this time, so many of them—including the Jemisons—moved north. Mae was three when her family arrived at the booming city of Chicago, which she thereafter considered her hometown.

Even there among the tall buildings, the smell of deep-dish pizza, and the sounds of jazz music pouring out of clubs, little Mae loved gazing up at the night sky. The twinkling stars mesmerized her not just then, but for the rest of her life.

Her parents nurtured this curiosity and encouraged Mae and her two siblings to ask questions and explore the world around them. If you don't know what a word means, you look it up—that's how Mae began to learn about the importance of research and self-reliance. The entire family regularly talked about politics, social issues, and community. They also talked about the **Civil Rights movement** and slavery.

"You can be anything you want," they told all three children.

Here in Chicago, Mae's parents found solid jobs—her father was a maintenance supervisor, and after going back to college, her mother was an elementary school teacher—and they were happy, kind, responsible, and smart. Of course, Mae believed them.

So, when her kindergarten teacher asked the class what they wanted to be when they grew up, Mae raised her hand up high and stated, "I want to be a scientist!" Her teacher tried to talk her into becoming a nurse, but Mae wasn't going to listen.

She knew in her heart that she was destined to be a scientist, even if others didn't believe in her.

It helped that her childhood was full of pets. They had dogs and even a rabbit, but Mae especially loved cats. "Cats have these remarkable superpowers of being able to be self-confident, resilient, and flexible," she said. Perhaps the cats in her life helped her learn those skills, too!

As a young Black girl in the 1960s, plenty of others told Mae that girls—especially Black girls—couldn't become astronauts. "Impossible!" many said. But Mae's determination was stronger than any doubters, and she never let their negativity bring her down.

Despite facing obstacles, Mae remained **undeterred**. Both in and outside of class, she devoured books about astronomy, physics, and chemistry, always eager to learn more about the universe and her place in it. Her curiosity was **insatiable**, and she eagerly shared her love for science with her friends and classmates. This young dreamer was on a mission to learn everything she could about the universe.

Mae's interests didn't stop at science, though. She had serious dance skills, too, and could twirl, leap, and spin with the best of them! Mae studied ballet, jazz, and African dance, often practicing for hours on end. She believed that science and dance were both ways to explore and understand the world, and she didn't see why she couldn't excel in both.

Like so many kids, TV played a role in Mae's

life. One of her favorite memories was watching the *Apollo 11* moon landing on TV in 1969. As Neil Armstrong took his historic first steps on the lunar surface, Mae thought, "One day, I want to do that, too!" She was just 12 years old at the time, but her dream of becoming an astronaut had already taken flight.

Mae also loved *Star Trek*, but even more so when her favorite character, Lieutenant Uhura, was on screen. Uhura was a role model for Mae because she was a strong, smart, and fearless

Black woman who broke barriers in the realm of science fiction. Mae knew she wanted to be like Uhura and make her mark on the world.

As much as Mae loved reading science fiction novels, it'd always made her angry how all the women were supporting characters. They weren't scientists, adventurers, or heroes. Why not? she wondered again and again.

Uhura gave her—and a generation of young Black girls—hope.

Of course, Mae was also a bright student who excelled in the public school system, where she consistently earned top grades and demonstrated a natural talent for problem-solving and critical thinking. Her teachers were amazed by her intelligence and drive.

The hard work and dedication paid off. She graduated from Morgan Park High School at the young age of 16 and set her sights on attending college! Mae received scholarship offers from every college she applied to, including the **prestigious** Stanford University. This was just the beginning of her incredible journey, and Mae's passion for learning would continue to guide her throughout her life.

WORDS TO KNOW

Civil Rights movement: A time between the 1950s and 1960s when people joined together to fight for fairness and equality for all, regardless of their race.

undeterred: Continuing to pursue a goal despite hardships or setbacks.

insatiable: An appetite or desire that is impossible to satisfy; always wanting more.

prestigious: Something respected and admired by many people.

THE WORLD AT THE TIME

In 1959:

- *The Wizard of Oz* is shown on TV for the first time.
- Hawaii becomes the 50th state.
- Russia's *Luna 3* space probe takes the first pictures of the far side of the moon.

WHAT DO YOU THINK?

- While looking for science books in the library, Mae stumbled across science fiction novels and fell in love. Why do you imagine these stories appealed to her?

- Gang violence was the norm for some of the places Mae lived in Chicago. "At night, occasionally, one would hear a popping sound, possibly shots," Mae wrote in her memoir, *Find Where the Wind Goes.* "Rule: turn off the lights and hit the floor until everything was over for at least 5 to 10 minutes." How do you think this kind of experience affected her?

3

A Stellar Education: The Launchpad for Success

I knew full well that people expected me to behave in a certain way. I bucked the system.

—MAE JEMISON

Let's zoom ahead to 1973, when a bright-eyed 16-year-old Mae arrives at Stanford

University. Her bags are packed with clothes she'd sewed herself, her dreams are as big as the heavens above, and she's ready to take the world by storm! Can you believe it? While most of us are still navigating high school, Mae's already heading off to college!

Why did she choose Stanford? Because they had a great engineering program and a massive

radio telescope. Plus, other people who'd attended that school had gone on to do amazing things, and that was her plan, too. Here's a brief list of some of its most famous **alumni**.

- Tiger Woods, one of the most successful golfers ever.
- Phil Knight, cofounder of Nike.
- Sundar Pichai, CEO of Google.
- Larry Page, cofounder of Google.
- Reed Hastings, cofounder of Netflix.
- Sally Ride, the first American woman in space.

Yeah, this is where Mae belonged.

As a first-year student, Mae decided to double-major in chemical engineering and African and Afro-American studies. She was a force to be reckoned with in the classroom, fearlessly tackling difficult subjects and soaking up knowledge like a sponge. But college wasn't just about hitting the books for Mae. She made time to get involved in campus life.

Mae also served as the head of the Black Students Union, advocating for diversity and equal opportunities on campus. She was passionate about creating a more inclusive environment where students from all backgrounds could thrive. Her efforts didn't go unnoticed. Mae became a prominent figure on campus, known for her leadership, intelligence, and commitment to social justice.

Now, this might seem surprising, but part of the reason she chose Stanford was because they had coed **intramural** football teams. She liked college football and wanted to get in on the action. So, Mae gave intramural football a shot and even played after getting a broken finger in the middle of a game. "It hurt like crazy, but I kept playing," she said. "This was too much fun!"

Another of Mae's favorite extracurricular activities was dancing with the Stanford dance troupe L'Academie. She gracefully glided across the stage with the team, twirling and leaping to the rhythm of the music. She even choreographed

a musical called *Out of the Shadows* during her freshman year. Talk about a multi-talented superstar!

While it was a wondrous time for Mae to be in such a creative environment, it wasn't all smooth sailing. She often found herself as the only woman or person of color in her classes. Can you imagine how isolated and alone that made her feel? Still, she was determined to succeed. She faced adversity head-on, challenging **stereotypes** and proving that she belonged in the world of **academia** just as much as anyone else.

Her goal was to change the perception of what women could and couldn't do. That meant speaking up and standing her ground. She wasn't just there for herself; she was also representing other women and people of color who had been overlooked and underestimated for too long. Mae knew that by succeeding at Stanford, she was breaking down barriers and opening doors for others like her.

In 1977, Mae graduated from Stanford with a Bachelor of Science in Chemical Engineering and a Bachelor of Arts in African and Afro-American Studies. She was ready to take on the next chapter in her incredible journey. What would that be? It was a coin flip—attend medical school or become a professional dancer. As smart as she was in science, she was just as gifted at dancing. Imagine that!

Her interest in medicine won out, so Mae headed to Cornell University in Ithaca, New York to attend medical school, where she continued to excel academically and break down barriers. But her journey was far from over. In fact, her greatest adventure was still to come.

WORDS TO KNOW

alumni: People who attended or graduated from a particular school, college, or university.

intramural: Games or sports that you play with people from your own community, instead of competing with other schools or groups.

stereotype: Overgeneralized ideas about a group of people, which can lead to unfair judgments or assumptions about them.

academia: The community of educators and educational institutions.

THE WORLD AT THE TIME

In 1973:

- Dr. Martin Cooper, a Motorola researcher, makes the world's first handheld mobile call on a phone the size of a brick.
- the World Trade Center in New York City is completed.
- Skylab, the United States' first space station, is launched.

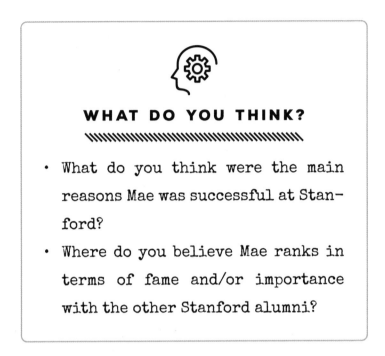

WHAT DO YOU THINK?

- What do you think were the main reasons Mae was successful at Stanford?
- Where do you believe Mae ranks in terms of fame and/or importance with the other Stanford alumni?

4

Healing Hands: The Earthly Adventures of Dr. Mae Jemison

You have the right to be involved. You have something important to contribute, and you have to take the risk to contribute it.

—MAE JEMISON

Before Mae Jemison became a household name as an astronaut, she was already a superhero in her own right: a medical doctor with healing hands and a heart of gold. Her journey into the world of medicine began when she entered Cornell Medical College in 1977. It's safe to say that Mae's passion for helping others was just as strong as her love for space.

While Mae's days at Cornell were filled with lectures, labs, late-night study sessions, and the occasional pickup basketball game for exercise, she still found time to continue her love for dance, attending classes at the Alvin Ailey American Dance Theater in New York City. Talk about being a multitasker!

In the summer after her second year of med school, she received a study grant to go to Kenya and help in clinics and hospitals. She also performed health surveys and even assisted in surgeries with The Flying Doctors—a team of doctors who went to areas so remote that the only way to get there was by plane!

On the way back to school from Kenya, Mae spent two weeks traveling through Egypt,

Greece, and Israel. No matter where she went, she found people, languages, and cultures fascinating.

It's worth noting that by this time, she could speak Russian, Japanese, and Swahili. Yeah, she has serious language skills!

Mae also said yes to other chances to gain international experience. During her time in medical school, she traveled to Cuba to conduct a study on Cuban healthcare, and she spent time in Thailand working at a Cambodian refugee camp. These experiences helped shape her worldview and her commitment to using her skills and knowledge to make a positive impact on global health.

After four years of hard work and dedication, Mae earned her Doctor of Medicine degree in 1981. She moved to Los Angeles to begin her medical career as a general practitioner. There, she provided medical care to people from all

walks of life, using her extensive knowledge and skills to treat patients and improve their health. She truly made a difference in her community, one patient at a time.

But Mae's biggest adventure was just around the corner. In 1983, she joined the Peace Corps, a volunteer program run by the United States government that sends Americans abroad to work on various projects in developing countries. Our hero is a **globetrotter**, too!

Mae's medical expertise landed her an assignment in West Africa, specifically Sierra Leone and Liberia. As a medical officer, she worked tirelessly to ensure that the volunteers were healthy and well taken care of, even in the most challenging conditions. She witnessed firsthand the struggles faced by people living in developing countries. From limited access to healthcare and education to the devastating effects of disease, Mae saw it all.

Her time in West Africa wasn't just about providing medical care; she also worked on research

projects focused on improving healthcare in the region. One of her most significant projects involved creating a vaccination program for children in rural Kenya. Thanks to her efforts, countless kids received life-saving vaccines that might not have been available otherwise.

In her memoir, Mae wrote: "On call twenty-four hours a day, seven days a week for two-

and-a-half years, in a place that could be so unforgiving of mistakes, I gained flexibility, knowledge, interpersonal relationship skills, and an appreciation of the challenges life poses to so many people on this planet."

Mae's time in the Peace Corps not only allowed her to help others, but it also reignited her childhood dream of reaching for the stars. In 1983, fellow Stanford **alumnus** Sally Ride became the first American woman in space, and this momentous event had a profound impact on Mae. She realized that it was time to turn her sky-high dreams into a reality. She decided to apply to NASA's astronaut program.

WORDS TO KNOW

globetrotter: A person who travels to many different countries around the world.

alumnus: The singular version of "alumni"—people who attended or graduated from a particular school, college, or university.

interstellar: What's happening in the big space between stars, like traveling or exploring the universe.

THE WORLD AT THE TIME

In 1977:

- the first *Star Wars* movie, *A New Hope,* is released in theaters.

- the first Apple II personal computer becomes available in stores.
- NASA launches the *Voyager* space probe to study the outer solar system and explore **interstellar** space.

WHAT DO YOU THINK?

- Which career seems harder—being a doctor or an astronaut? Which would you rather do?
- How do you think Mae's medical background and experiences as a doctor contributed to her journey as an astronaut?

5

Countdown to Space: Becoming an Astronaut

Some people say they feel very small when they think about space. I felt more expansive, very connected to the universe.

—MAE JEMISON

Mae Jemison had always dreamt of going to space, but to make that happen, she had to apply to NASA's astronaut program. In 1985, Mae decided it was finally time to take the plunge and submitted her application. Thousands of highly qualified individuals from all over the country applied, but only a select few would be chosen to join the elite ranks of NASA astronauts.

Then one of the biggest tragedies in the history of space exploration happened. In 1986, the *Challenger* space shuttle exploded 73 seconds after liftoff. The world was devastated, and NASA put a hold on everything, including the selection of new candidates for its astronaut program.

Science eventually provided an answer to what happened—a design flaw caused the *Challenger*'s O-ring to fail. After the design was corrected and NASA was convinced that future space shuttles would be safe, they began moving forward again.

After several nail-biting months, Mae received the news she had been hoping for: she was one of about 100 people invited to interview at NASA's Johnson Space Center in Houston,

Texas! Excited and **resolute**, Mae prepared for this once-in-a-lifetime opportunity. Not everyone who went to NASA actually earned the chance to go to space, but Mae knew she could do this. She'd been preparing for it her whole life.

During the interview process, Mae faced a series of rigorous tests and evaluations. These assessments were designed to determine her physical fitness, mental aptitude, and ability to

work well under pressure. She also participated in group exercises to evaluate her teamwork skills, a crucial trait for astronauts who would spend weeks or even months together in the confined area of a spacecraft. How does that sound to you?

Despite the intense competition, Mae's background in medicine, her experience working in remote locations with the Peace Corps, and her unwavering passion for space exploration set her apart from the crowd. In June 1987, Mae received the incredible news: she had been selected as one of the fifteen astronaut candidates in her class! Her dream of reaching the stars was one step closer to becoming a reality.

But before Mae could strap on her space boots and blast off into orbit, she now had to complete a grueling year of astronaut training at the Johnson Space Center. This training would prepare her for the physical, mental, and emotional challenges of space travel, ensuring she was ready to take on whatever the **cosmos** had in store.

Mae's astronaut training covered a wide range of topics, from learning the intricacies of spacecraft systems and operations to mastering the art of extravehicular activity (EVA), also known as spacewalking. She also received extensive training in robotics, allowing her to operate the space

shuttle's robotic arm, a vital tool for deploying satellites and performing other tasks in orbit.

To prepare for the unique experience of living and working in microgravity, Mae underwent training in NASA's "Weightless Wonder," a specially modified airplane that simulates the feeling of weightlessness by flying in steep **arcs**. This allowed her to practice moving and working in an environment without gravity, a critical skill for any astronaut.

But Mae's training wasn't just about learning to function in space; it also focused on survival skills for emergency situations. She learned how to survive in extreme environments, such as the ocean or a desert, in case her spacecraft made an unexpected landing. She also trained in emergency medical procedures, firefighting techniques, and other vital skills that could make the difference between life and death in a crisis. In space, you can't just call 911 for help!

In August 1988, she was officially designated an astronaut, making her one of the few who had

earned the right to wear the coveted NASA "astronaut wings."

It wasn't long before she got the news she had been waiting for: she was assigned to the STS-47 Spacelab J mission aboard the *Endeavour* space shuttle. The launch date was set for September 12, 1992, and Mae's heart brimmed with excitement as she prepared for the adventure of a lifetime.

WORDS TO KNOW

resolute: Unwavering in purpose or belief.

cosmos: The observable universe, including all matter and energy that exists.

arc: Move with a curving path.

THE WORLD AT THE TIME

In 1985:

- the first version of Microsoft Windows, Windows 1.0, is launched.
- Nintendo releases the revolutionary video game *Super Mario Bros.*
- Kathryn Sullivan becomes the first American woman to walk in space.

WHAT DO YOU THINK?

- Would the *Challenger* space shuttle disaster have changed your mind about going to space?
- What qualities do you think are most important for an astronaut candidate to possess?

6

Soaring into History: The STS-47 Mission

Science provides an understanding of a universal experience. Arts provide a universal understanding of a personal experience.

—MAE JEMISON

With her astronaut training complete, Mae eagerly awaited her chance to fly to space.

Finally, the big day arrived. NASA selected her to be a Mission Specialist on the *Endeavour* space shuttle for the STS-47 mission. Yet this was no ordinary mission; it was a cooperative venture between the United States and Japan, focusing on science experiments and Earth observation.

As the countdown to launch day began, Mae and her six crewmates prepared themselves for the journey of a lifetime. They spent countless

hours reviewing mission objectives, practicing experiments, and running through emergency procedures. Mae was assigned the important role of conducting experiments on how space travel affects the human body.

The anticipation was **palpable** on September 12, 1992, as Mae and her crewmates stood at the base of the massive *Endeavour* space shuttle, its gleaming white and black exterior towering above them. With their bright-orange launch suits on and helmets tucked under their arms, they looked like superheroes ready to conquer the universe.

Picture this exhilarating scene: Mae climbs into the shuttle, her heart pounding with exhilaration and anticipation. She straps herself into her seat, the hum of the spacecraft's systems filling her ears. The countdown begins, and with each number, the tension builds.

"10 . . . 9 . . . 8 . . . "

The engines ignite with a roar. Mae is oh-so-ready to go!

"3 . . . 2 . . . 1 . . . Liftoff!"

7.7 million pounds of thrust accelerates the *Endeavor* into the sky, taking it from zero to 17,500 miles per hour in mere moments! The shuttle soars up and up, leaving behind a trail of smoke and fire as it hurtles toward the stars. Mae is on her way!

As the shuttle races through Earth's atmosphere, the force of gravity tugging on Mae's body slowly fades away. And then, suddenly, she's floating! Mae and her crewmates are now experiencing the incredible sensation of weightlessness, a feeling that's both thrilling and disorienting. Imagine trying to eat, sleep, or even brush your teeth while floating in midair!

Mae and her crewmates worked tirelessly to conduct a variety of experiments. Mae's primary responsibility was studying the effects of space

on the human body, specifically focusing on the **vestibular system**, which helps us keep our balance. She performed tests on her fellow astronauts and even on herself, contributing valuable data to our understanding of how humans adapt to the weightlessness of space. She even got to speak to students on Earth via a live video link, sharing her experiences and inspiring young minds to dream big.

But it wasn't all work and no play for Mae and her crew. They also found time to marvel at the breathtaking views of Earth from the shuttle's windows. Imagine Mae, her face pressed against the glass, staring down at our planet from 190 miles above. The blues, greens, and browns of Earth's surface blend together like an **Impressionist** painting, while the thin, blue veil of the atmosphere hugs the planet's curve. It's a sight few people have ever witnessed, and for Mae, it was a dream come true.

She couldn't help but dance a little, too, twirling gracefully in zero gravity.

After eight unforgettable days orbiting Earth, it was time for Mae and her crew to return home. The shuttle's engines roared to life once more, propelling the spacecraft back toward Earth. As they re-entered the atmosphere, friction between the shuttle and the air created a spectacular light show outside the windows. The superheated air crackled and streaked past like shooting stars, signaling their impending return to solid ground.

With a gentle thud, the *Endeavour* space shuttle touched down on the runway, bringing Mae and her crewmates safely back to Earth. They had traveled over 3.2 million miles and orbited our planet 127 times during their journey.

As they exited the shuttle, the reality of their incredible accomplishment began to sink in. Mae Jemison had made history as the first Black woman in space, but some of her crewmates made history, too. Mamoru Mohri was the shuttle's first Japanese astronaut, and Mark Lee and Jan Davis became the first married couple to fly on the same space mission. Talk about a truly historic trip!

Mae's spaceflight, though, not only broke barriers, but it also inspired countless young people to believe in themselves and reach for the stars by pursuing careers in science, technology, engineering, and math (STEM). Her fearless pursuit of her dreams, even in the face of adversity, serves as a shining example for future generations to follow.

WORDS TO KNOW

palpable: So intense or strong that it can be felt or sensed, even if not touched.

vestibular system: The parts of the inner ear and brain that help control balance, orientation, and spatial awareness.

Impressionism: An art movement from the late 19th century where artists tried to capture the feeling or "impression" of a moment.

THE WORLD AT THE TIME

In 1993:

- Disney's animated film *Aladdin* is a smash hit.
- the Hubble Space Telescope takes its first clear image of a distant galaxy.
- the World Wide Web (www) becomes free for everyone to use.

WHAT DO YOU THINK?

- What do you think was the most memorable moment of the STS-47 mission for Mae and her crewmates?

- On her journey to space, Mae brought a few special items, including a Bundu statue from a women's society in Sierra Leone and an Alvin Ailey Dance Theater poster featuring Black dancer Judith Jamison. What especially meaningful things would you bring if you were going to space?

7

Lights, Camera, Action! Mae Takes on Hollywood

There have been lots of other women who had the talent and ability before me. And I hope it means I'm just the first in a long line.

—MAE JEMISON

Hold onto your popcorn, space fans. In this star-studded chapter, we're going to explore how Mae Jemison rocketed her way from the cosmos to the big screen. That's right, our favorite astronaut has made her mark in Hollywood, too!

After her journey to space, Mae's life became even more exciting. She'd already broken barriers in the world of science, but she was about to make history in a whole new way: by becoming the first real astronaut to appear on the iconic sci-fi TV series, *Star Trek*!

Mae had been a fan of *Star Trek* since she was a little girl. The show's vision of a diverse, harmonious future where people of all races worked together to explore the stars inspired her own dreams of becoming an astronaut. And it wasn't just any *Star Trek* character that captured her imagination—it was Lieutenant Uhura, played by the fabulous Nichelle Nichols, who showed young Mae that a Black woman could be an essential part of a space crew.

Fast forward to Mae's time in space: the crew of the *Endeavour* space shuttle knew about her love for *Star Trek*, and they even made a playful announcement when she beamed a greeting to the Earth: "Hailing frequencies open!"

As the communications officer for the USS *Enterprise*, Uhura often used the term "hailing frequencies." How cool is that?

But Mae's *Star Trek* adventure didn't end there. After her mission, she was invited to make a special guest appearance on *Star Trek: The Next Generation*. In the 1993 episode "Second Chances," Mae played Lieutenant Palmer, a

transporter operator who helped the crew of the starship *Enterprise* navigate a tricky situation. Talk about a fantasy fufilled!

Being on the set of *Star Trek* was an out-of-this-world experience for Mae. She got to rub elbows with the show's stars like Patrick Stewart, who played Captain Jean-Luc Picard, and LeVar Burton, who portrayed Lieutenant Commander Geordi La Forge. And she even had a heartwarming moment with Nichelle Nichols—Uhura herself!—who visited the set to meet Mae and pass on the torch of inspiration.

Mae's appearance on *Star Trek* wasn't just a fun **cameo**, though. It was a powerful symbol of how far she'd come and how much she'd achieved. By stepping onto the set of her favorite show, Mae proved that the ambitions we have as kids can come true if we work hard and believe in ourselves.

But Mae's impact on Hollywood didn't end with *Star Trek*. She's also been an advisor on various space-themed films, sharing her expertise to make sure the movies are as scientifically accurate as possible while still being thrilling. She even consulted on the movie *Mars Attacks!*—a wacky sci-fi comedy that's a far cry from her real-life experience in space!

Mae's **foray** into Hollywood is proof of her incredible **versatility** and her passion for inspiring others. By sharing her story and lending her expertise to the world of entertainment, she's helped countless young people see themselves as future astronauts, scientists, and engineers.

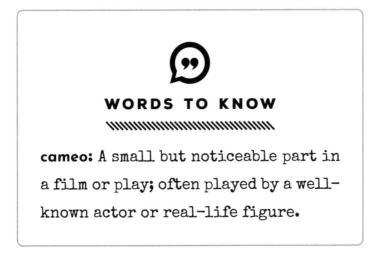

WORDS TO KNOW

cameo: A small but noticeable part in a film or play; often played by a well-known actor or real-life figure.

foray: An attempt to do something in a new or different field or area.

versatility: The ability to adapt to many different functions or activities; being good at many different things.

THE WORLD AT THE TIME

In 1993:

- Kim Campbell becomes Canada's first female prime minister.
- the first online web browser, Mosaic, is launched.
- the pilot for *Bill Nye the Science Guy* is a hit and the series becomes one of the most watched educational TV shows in the United States.

WHAT DO YOU THINK?

- What TV show would you love to have a cameo appearance on?
- If you were to collaborate with Mae on a film or TV project, what would it be about?

8

Building a Legacy: The Jemison Foundation and the 100 Year Starship Project

The future never just happened. It was created.

—MAE JEMISON

After her incredible journey to space, you might think Mae Jemison would take it easy for a while. But if there's one thing we've learned about her, it's that she's always ready for the next adventure! Let's explore Mae's post-astronaut life, where she continues to inspire future generations through her passion for education, advocacy, and innovation with her foundation and the 100 Year Starship project.

The Dorothy Jemison Foundation for Excellence, named in honor of her mother, was established by Mae in 1994. The foundation's mission is to foster a love for science and learning among young people, especially those from underrepresented groups. Through various programs and **initiatives**, the foundation aims to empower students and provide them with the tools and resources needed to pursue STEM careers.

Now, let's jump ahead to examine Mae's most ambitious project yet because it's a gamechanger. Let's be clear—this is about as ambitious as a project gets.

The 100 Year Starship (100YSS) is a mind-blowing idea. The project, initiated by the Defense Advanced Research Projects Agency (DARPA) and NASA, aimed to develop the technology necessary for interstellar travel within the next 100 years. In 2012, the Dorothy Jemison Foundation for Excellence was awarded

a $500,000 grant by DARPA to manage the project, and Mae was appointed as the project's principal investigator.

Mae's role as the leader of this futuristic project is no surprise. She's always been passionate about exploring the universe and using science to make the world a better place. And with the 100 Year Starship, she's proving that no dream is too big—even if it involves traveling light years away from Earth!

But what does it actually take to build a starship that can carry humans to another solar system? Well, it's not as simple as packing a few sandwiches and blasting off. There are tons of challenges to overcome, from finding a suitable destination to developing advanced propulsion systems and figuring out how to keep astronauts healthy, happy, and safe during a long voyage through the heavens.

One of the main goals of the 100YSS is to spark innovation and encourage research in various fields, such as energy, propulsion, materials, and life support. By tackling these challenges head-on, the project aims to make groundbreaking discoveries that will not only help us reach the stars but also improve life right here on Earth. Talk about a win-win!

Another important aspect of the 100 Year Starship is its focus on **inclusivity** and diversity. Mae believes that the best way to solve problems and make breakthroughs is by bringing together people from all walks of life, with different skills, perspectives, and backgrounds. And she's made it her mission to ensure that everyone has a seat at the table, from young students to seasoned experts.

To help inspire the next generation of space enthusiasts, the 100YSS also organizes events and workshops where kids can learn about the wonders of the universe and the importance of working together to achieve our wildest goals. Who knows, maybe you could be part of the team that makes history by launching the first-ever human mission to another star!

Mae Jemison's passion for space exploration knows no bounds. With the 100 Year Starship, she's challenging us all to reach for the stars—literally!

So, whether you're an aspiring astronaut, a curious scientist, or a creative thinker who loves to dream big, there's something for everyone in the amazing world of the 100 Year Starship. And with Mae Jemison at the helm, there's no telling what incredible adventures await us in the great cosmic beyond!

WORDS TO KNOW

initiatives: Plans, projects, or programs created to achieve a specific goal.

inclusivity: The practice of including people of all backgrounds, cultures, and abilities.

THE WORLD AT THE TIME

In 2012:

- *The Hunger Games* movie—based on the popular book series—is a global sensation.
- the *Curiosity* rover successfully lands on Mars, beginning its mission to explore the planet's surface and search for signs of life.
- Felix Baumgartner completes the Red Bull Stratos project, breaking the sound barrier during his free-fall from the edge of space.

WHAT DO YOU THINK?

- What is the most exciting aspect of the 100 Year Starship project?

- Pretend you have the opportunity to interview Mae Jemison for a podcast or YouTube channel. What fun and interesting questions would you ask her to entertain and engage your audience?

9

Sharing the Universe: Mae as Author, Speaker, and Storyteller

The arts and sciences are avatars
of human creativity.

—MAE JEMISON

After her mind-blowing adventure on the Space Shuttle *Endeavour*, Mae was determined to share her enthusiasm for space and science with curious youngsters. So, she swapped her spacesuit for a teacher's cap and launched her new mission on Earth: making a difference in education.

Mae headed to the classroom, where she became a professor of environmental studies at Dartmouth College. There, she ignited her students' imaginations with her tales of space travel and her passion for preserving our beautiful planet. In this role, she not only taught them about science and the environment but also inspired them to chase their wildest dreams.

But Mae's influence didn't stop there! She's also the author of several fantastic books, including *Find Where the Wind Goes: Moments from My Life*, a 1992 autobiography that she updated in 2020. It chronicles her awe-inspiring journey from a young dreamer to a history-making astronaut. Her writing captures the hearts and minds of readers, motivating them to strive for their goals and never give up.

Mae's also a sought-after speaker, traveling to schools and conferences worldwide to share her incredible story and inspire the next generation of space enthusiasts. Imagine sitting in your classroom, and suddenly, an actual astronaut walks in to talk about her own journey to space! Now that's a guest speaker you'll never forget.

As an advocate for STEM education, Mae founded the Mae Jemison Science Reading Room in Chicago, a place where young learners can explore the world of science through books and hands-on activities. This magical place helps kids to develop a love for learning and the confidence to pursue their passion for STEM.

Mae's foundation also created The Earth We Share (TEWS), an international science camp for kids aged 12 to 16. At TEWS, students from around the world come together to solve real-world problems using science, technology,

engineering, and math skills. The camp encourages teamwork, creative thinking, and problem-solving, helping to shape the next generation of STEM leaders. Undoubtedly, it's sparked countless space-loving dreams in the hearts of its participants. Pretty terrific, right?

So, what's the secret to Mae's success as an author, educator, and role model? It's her unwavering belief in the power of imagination and her contagious enthusiasm for exploration. As she once said, "The best way to make dreams come true is to wake up." Thanks to her amazing work, young dreamers everywhere are waking up to the boundless possibilities that await them in the realms of science, technology, engineering, and math.

Mae Jemison's impact as a mentor, author, and speaker stretches far beyond the Earth's atmosphere. With her guidance and inspiration, you can bet there'll be a whole new generation of space explorers eager to embark on their own stellar journeys.

THE WORLD AT THE TIME

In 2020:

- the COVID-19 pandemic impacts the world, leading to lockdowns and social distancing measures.
- SpaceX's *Dragon* becomes the first private spacecraft to send astronauts to the International Space Station.
- NASA launches the Mars 2020 mission, including the *Perseverance* rover and *Ingenuity* helicopter.

WHAT DO YOU THINK?

- If you were to attend one of Mae's speaking events, what topic would you be most interested in hearing about?
- What should Mae's next book be about?

10

Mae Jemison: The Astronaut Who Changed the World

Don't let anyone rob you of your imagination,
your creativity, or your curiosity.

—MAE JEMISON

But wait, there's more—Mae's passion for space doesn't stop at the stars. She's also a major advocate for the Earth! She believes that exploring the cosmos can teach us important lessons about protecting our home planet. After all, when you're floating high above Earth, you can't help but realize how interconnected everything is.

That's why Mae's committed to using space technology for good. From satellites that monitor climate change to robots that clean up space debris, she's always looking for ways to apply her out-of-this-world knowledge to make our planet a better place for future generations.

And speaking of future generations, Mae's got big dreams for the young space enthusiasts out there. As a teacher, mentor, and founder of her very own foundation, she's dedicated to inspiring kids to go after an amazing for themselves, just like she did.

In fact, the Dorothy Jemison Foundation for Excellence supports as range of educational programs that encourage young people to dive into the exciting world of STEM. Mae wants to make sure that every kid, no matter their background, has the opportunity to explore the wonders of the science while achieving their full potential.

Mae's influence also extends to collaborating with companies and organizations that share her vision for a better future. By partnering with these groups, she helps create opportunities for

innovation, research, and education in space exploration and STEM fields.

Through her foundation and various partnerships, Mae has developed initiatives to promote environmental **stewardship** and sustainable living. These projects inspire people of all ages to be mindful of their impact on the Earth and to make choices that protect our precious planet.

So, what does Mae's ideal future look like? Imagine a world where kids from all walks of life work together to build the next generation of spaceships, design cutting-edge space habitats, and discover mind-boggling new planets. It's a world where astronauts of all colors and genders embark on epic adventures to distant stars, unlocking the mysteries of the universe and expanding humanity's horizons.

In her quest to inspire young minds, Mae has even ventured into the realm of entertainment, using her unique experiences to help shape stories that spark curiosity and ignite the imagination. This fusion of science and storytelling creates a powerful tool for inspiring future generations to strive for greatness.

And guess what? With innovators like Mae Jemison leading the way, that future could be closer than you think! As long as we keep dreaming big, working together, and pushing the boundaries of what's possible, there's no telling where tomorrow might take us.

In the wise words of Mae herself: "I learned never to be limited by other people's limited imagination. And never to limit others due to the limits of my own imagination." So, let's follow in her space-boot prints and dare to chase out-of-this-world dreams. Who knows? One day, you might just find yourself soaring among the stars, too!

WORDS TO KNOW

stewardship: The act or process of preserving something, such as natural resources or the environment.

exoplanet: A planet outside our solar system.

THE WORLD AT THE TIME

In 2023:

- the James Webb Space Telescope has replaced the Hubble Space Telescope because of its ability to observe infrared light and to detect chemicals in the atmospheres of distant **exoplanets.**

- the Artemis III mission aims to land astronauts, including the first woman, on the Moon.
- the European Space Agency's JUICE mission plans to study Jupiter's icy moons.

WHAT DO YOU THINK?

- In 2017, LEGO created a fan-inspired project, Women of NASA, which includes astronomer and educator Nancy Grace Roman; computer scientist and entrepreneur Margaret Hamilton; astronaut, physicist and entrepreneur Sally Ride; and astronaut, physician, and engineer Mae Jemison. What other women scientists deserve to be immortalized in LEGO sets?

- If you were to write a comic book or graphic novel starring Mae Jemison as a superhero, what would her superhero name be, and what powers or gadgets would she have to save the world or explore the universe?

Glossary

academia—The community of educators and educational institutions.

alumni—People who attended or graduated from a particular school, college, or university.

alumnus—The singular version of "alumni"— people who attended or graduated from a particular school, college, or university.

arc—Move with a curving trajectory.

cameo—A small but noticeable part in a film or play, often played by a well-known actor or real-life figure.

Civil Rights movement—A time between the 1950s and 1960s when people joined together to fight for fairness and equality for all, regardless of their race.

cosmos—The observable universe, including all matter and energy that exists.

exoplanet—A planet outside our Solar System.

foray—An attempt to do something in a new or different field or area.

globetrotter—A person who travels to many different countries around the world.

Impressionism—An art movement from the late 19th century where artists tried to capture the feeling or "impression" of a moment.

inclusivity—The practice of including people of all backgrounds, cultures, and abilities.

initiatives—Plans, projects, or programs created to achieve a specific goal.

innovative—Introducing new ideas; being creative and original.

insatiable—An appetite or desire that is impossible to satisfy; always wanting more.

interstellar—What's happening in the big space between stars, like traveling or exploring the universe.

intramural—Games or sports that you play with people from your own community, instead of competing with other schools or groups.

palpable—So intense or strong that it can be felt or sensed, even if not touched.

prestigious—Something respected and admired by many people.

resolute—Unwavering in purpose or belief.

stewardship—The act or process of preserving something, such as natural resources or the environment.

stereotype—Overgeneralized ideas about a group of people, which can lead to unfair judgments or assumptions about them.

trailblazer—A person who makes a new track through wild country or is the first to do something exciting or different.

undeterred—Continuing to pursue a goal despite hardships or setbacks.

vestibular system—The parts of the inner ear and brain that help control balance, orientation, and spatial awareness.

versatility—The ability to adapt to many different functions or activities; being good at many different things.

Timeline

1956: Born October 17 in Decatur, Alabama

1959: Family moves to Chicago, Illinois

1973: Attends Stanford University at age 16

1980: Works as a medical office for the Peace Corps

1981: Graduates from Cornell Medical School

1987: Accepted into NASA's astronaut training program

1992: *Endeavor* space shuttle launches on September 12

1993: Receives the Kilby Science Award

1993: Is the first astronaut to be a guest actor on *Star Trek*

1994: Established the Dorothy Jemison Foundation for Excellence

1994: Establishes The Earth We Share (TEWS) international space camp

1995: Becomes a professor of Environmental Studies at Dartmouth College

1995: Founds Jemison Institute for Advancing Technologies in Developing Countries

1999: Publishes her autobiography *Find Where the Wind Goes: Moments from My Life*

2002: Receives the Rachel Carson Award for environmental awareness efforts

2004: Inducted into the International Space Hall of Fame

2010: Appointed to the National Academy of Sciences' Institute of Medicine

2012: Takes over the 100 Year Starship program

2017: Receives Buzz Aldrin Space Pioneer Award

Selected Bibliography

Gibbs, Nancy, "The Astronaut Who Will Change the Face of Space," *Time*, September 16, 1991.

Jemison, Mae. *Find Where the Wind Goes: Moments From My Life*. Houston: Signal Hill Road Publishing, 2022.

Jemison, Mae, and Dana Meachen Rau. *Mae Jemison: Out of This World*. Mankato, MN: Capstone Press, 2013.

Jemison, Mae, "Teach Arts and Sciences Together," Ted.com, 2002.

Nolen, Stephanie, "Astronaut Mae Jemison:

Coming in from Outer Space," *Ms. Magazine*, November/December 1992.

Smith, Mark, *Mae Jemison: An Extraordinary Life: The Journey, the Lesson, the Rules for Success*, MR, April 2021.

Williams, Alexis, "The Legacy of Mae Jemison, the First Black Woman to Travel Space," *Vice*, February 16, 2018.

About Chris Singleton

Chris Singleton is a former professional athlete drafted by the Chicago Cubs in 2017. Following the loss of his mother in a racially motivated mass shooting, Chris has now become an inspirational speaker and best-selling author who has shared his message of unity and racial reconciliation with NFL and NBA teams as well as multiple Fortune 500 companies across the country. He shares with over 100 organizations and over 30,000 students annually. He resides with his spouse, Mariana, and three children in Charleston, South Carolina.

About Ryan G. Van Cleave

Dr. Ryan G. Van Cleave is the author of dozens of fiction, nonfiction, and poetry books for both children and adults. When Ryan's not writing, he's crisscrossing the country, teaching writing at schools throughout the United States. He also moonlights as The Picture Book Whisperer™, helping celebrities write stories for kids and bring them to life on the page, stage, and screen.

Adriana Pérez Perales

Adriana is a freelance illustrator from Mexico. Her clients include Oxford University Press, Scholastic, Get Ready Comics, and many others.

MILK +
COOKIES

About Milk & Cookies

Milk & Cookies is the middle-grade imprint of Bushel & Peck Books, a children's publisher with a special mission. Through our Book-for-Book Promise™, we donate one book to kids in need for every book we sell. Our beautiful books are given to kids through schools, libraries, local neighborhoods, shelters, and nonprofits, and also to many selfless organizations that are working hard to make a difference. So thank you for purchasing this book! Because of you, another book will make its way into the hands of a child who needs it most. Do you know a school, a library, or an organization that could use some free books for their kids? We'd love to help! Please fill out the nomination form on our website, and we'll do everything we can to make something happen.